FLAVOURS SERIES

Fabulous
FISHCAKES

Elizabeth Feltham

Preface by
Ross Mavis and John Bishop

Formac Publishing Company Limited
Halifax

Formac Publishing Company Limited recognizes the support of the Province of Nova Scotia through the Department of Tourism, Culture and Heritage.

We acknowledge the financial support of the Government of Canada through the Book Publishing Industry Development Program (BPIDP) for our publishing activities.

National Library of Canada Cataloguing in Publication Data

Feltham, Elizabeth
     Fabulous fishcakes : recipes from Canada's best chefs / Elizabeth Feltham ; preface by Ross Mavis and John Bishop. -- 2nd ed.

(Flavours series)
Includes index.
ISBN 10: 0-88780-695-3   ISBN 13: 978-0-88780-695-7

     1. Cookery (Fish). 2. Cookery (Seafood). I. Title. II. Series.

TX747.F43 2006   641.6'92   C2005-907232-6

Formac Publishing Company Limited
5502 Atlantic Street
Halifax, Nova Scotia
B3H 1G4
www.formac.ca

Printed and bound in Canada

Contents

Fishcake Memories

As a child growing up in Britain my memory of fishcakes is that they were a regular meal in my home. Usually made with leftover cooked fish such as Atlantic cod, halibut or salmon, they were a way to stretch the budget. Combined with mashed potatoes and chopped parsley they were guaranteed to fill a boy's hungry stomach. How things have changed! The lowly fishcake has become a gastronomical delight at our restaurant. Consider the combinations of exotic ingredients available today — lemon grass, coconut and ginger, for example, will create a fishcake with an Asian flavour. At Bishop's we make our fishcakes using the freshest of seafood available; Dungeness crab or fresh hand-peeled shrimp combined with flakes of barbecued salmon. Yum!

And I'll let you in on a little secret. Use just enough breadcrumb or cracker filling to bind the cakes, as this allows the seafood to shine through.

—John Bishop
Bishop's Restaurant, Vancouver, BC

Anyone who thinks there could be little excitement in fishcakes is in for a big surprise. Although there are dozens of ways to make traditional fishcakes there are even more when untraditional, innovative ingredients are used. A quick browse through this cookbook will leave you with a greater respect for the humble side dish.

Along with the variety of traditional salt cod and potato recipes you might expect, there are also those containing fresh salmon, smoked salmon and sablefish. Added to these are recipes for shellfishcakes of Dungeness crab, snow crab, shrimp, lobster, prawns and scallops.

How did the lowly fishcake get its start? For those of us living on either coast of Canada the answer is an obvious one. Fish of all kinds have always been a valuable source of protein, fats, minerals and vitamins in our diet. Salmon and the silvery euchalon, a smelt-like fish, were originally harvested by West Coast Indians while Atlantic salmon, gaspereau and capelin were taken on the East Coast by its indigenous peoples. From that time on, salmon, herring, cod, haddock and halibut, plus many species of freshwater fish, became a food staple that graced tables throughout Canada and the rest of the world. Imagination was all that was needed to mix and mash leftover fish and potatoes from the night before into pan-sized cakes for crispy frying the next day.

Before I became a professional chef in New Brunswick, I cooked throughout BC and Yukon before moving to Toronto and from there to the Maritimes. The staple mashed potato and fish pancake has accompanied me across the country. In the modest galley of my Thunderbird sloop, anchored off north Vancouver Island, I loved the sizzling sound of smoked salmon fishcakes warming up for supper. Another of my favourites was Greyling fishcakes prepared in a cast-iron frying pan over an open fire on the marge of Lac Labarge, Yukon. Kokanee (landlocked salmon) formed into fishcakes made crispy from melted butter were gourmet fare while camping with my Doukhabor friends in Castlegar, BC. In the east I discovered Walleye fishcakes as a lakeshore lunch in northern Ontario and now, beside the majestic Bay of Fundy, I relish haddock and salt cod fishcakes as often as I wish.

In Atlantic Canada, salt cod was considered a basic staple in many households for years. No respectable pantry would be without a side or two of dried salt cod and several tins of canned haddock, called Finnan Haddie. When my wife joined me in Toronto to spend a few years away from the Maritimes, she arrived with Finnan Haddie and several bags of salt cod pieces for fishcakes.

One of the most important attributes of any good chef, either commercial or domestic, is the power of imagination. Great examples of taking the humble fishcake and turning it into a work of art can be found in this cookbook. Today's menus are a blend of local and international ingredients and traditional and innovative ideas. Wasabi horseradish, familiar to all who know

sushi like I know sushi, curry mango mayonnaise, jalapeño peppers, organic tomato ketchup, chipotle lime juice and lemon aïoli all are part of the interracial marriage now consummated with fishcakes. I commend all these recipes to you and encourage you to experience the world of fabulous fishcakes. Never forget, however, one of the most satisfying aspects of a humble fishcake: it is versatile. When sexy ingredients are unavailable, you can still make a delicious meal using cooked fish, an egg for binding, potatoes and seasoning. To gild the lily, we in the Maritimes add a spoonful of green tomato relish, called chow chow, to our plates. Nestle a hot crispy fishcake next to a spoonful of home-baked beans, a couple of slices of thick fried bacon and a slice of crusty brown bread and voilà, you have a meal fit for royalty.

—Ross Mavis
Inn on the Cove, Saint John, NB

Salmon

Almost all commercially available Atlantic salmon is now farmed and, despite hot debate, advances in aquaculture result in excellent fish with very little taste difference from the wild. There are five species of Pacific salmon, most still caught wild.

The rich, buttery flavour of salmon is indicative of its high oil content. Any of the salmon types, fresh or frozen, will yield excellent fishcakes. When buying whole fish, look for shiny scales and bright eyes. If the fish is already filleted, check for smell — there shouldn't be a strong fishy aroma. When buying frozen, beware of signs of freezer burn or frost in the package. Canned salmon is not recommended for these recipes, but could be experimented with in a pinch.

Salmon Cakes

Blomidon Inn, Wolfville, NS

Chef Sean Laceby says that fresh ingredients always give the best results. He also says it is important to put the breadcrumb coating on at the last minute, just before frying: "This really helps to give a crisp exterior and to keep the flavour at its best." This is one of the inn's most popular dishes.

12 oz (340 g) salmon, boneless fillets
1 cup (250 mL) mashed potatoes
  (½ lb/225 g/ about 5 medium peeled potatoes)
1 egg, lightly beaten
¼ cup (50 mL) sour cream
½ cup (125 mL) fresh breadcrumbs
1 tbsp (15 mL) fresh dill
2 tsp (10 mL) salt
1 tsp (5 mL) pepper
For breading:
½ cup (125 mL) fresh breadcrumbs
For cooking:
vegetable oil

Bring saucepan or deep skillet of water to boil; turn heat to medium and place salmon in pan, ensuring water covers fish. Cook until salmon flakes apart easily, drain and let cool.

Peel and cube potatoes. In large pot, cover potatoes with cold water and bring to boil, cooking until easily pierced with knife. Drain and mash.

In large bowl, combine salmon, potatoes, egg, sour cream, breadcrumbs, dill, salt and pepper.

Mix well and form into patties. Coat with breadcrumbs.

Heat vegetable oil in skillet over medium heat, add cakes and brown on both sides, turning once.

4 fishcakes / 2 servings

Suggested sauce: Hollandaise Sauce (see page 87)

Salmon and Wasabi fishcakes

Charlotte Lane Café, Shelburne, NS

"Even though it's not a traditional Maritime dish," says Kathleen Glauser, "this dish has gathered a real local following, especially with our Saturday brunch customers." She suggests serving it with a green salad.

1 cup (250 mL) mashed potatoes (½ lb/225 g/ about 5 medium peeled potatoes)
8 oz (225 g) salmon, skinless and boned
½ tsp (2 mL) olive oil
½ cup (125 mL) chopped red onions
1 tbsp (15 mL) chopped garlic
1 tbsp (15 mL) Worcestershire sauce
½ tsp (2 mL) dried dill
1 tsp (5 mL) salt
½ tsp (2 mL) pepper
1 tsp (5 mL) paprika
2 tsp (10 mL) wasabi powder
For breading:
½ to 1 cup (125 to 250 mL) flour
For cooking:
olive oil

Peel and cube potatoes. In a large pot, cover potatoes with cold water and bring to boil, cooking until easily pierced with knife. Drain and mash.

Bring saucepan or deep skillet of water to boil; turn heat to medium and place salmon in pan, ensuring water covers fish. Cook until salmon flakes apart easily, drain and let cool.

In frying pan, heat olive oil, sauté red onions and garlic until soft, remove from heat.

In large bowl, combine salmon, potatoes, red onions, garlic, Worcestershire sauce, dill, salt, pepper, paprika and wasabi.

Form into patties and refrigerate for several hours.

Dust with flour.

Fry in olive oil over medium heat until browned on both sides, turning once.

4 fishcakes / 2 servings

Suggested sauce: Curry Mango Mayonnaise (see page 10)

Salmon Cakes

Chanterelle Inn, North River, St. Anns Bay, NS

Chef Earlene Busch says the hake in this recipe acts as an emulsifier in place of the more traditional use of breadcrumbs or potato. This makes it an excellent choice for gluten-free diets.

5 oz (145 g) hake (or other white fish such as
   cod or haddock)
1 tsp (5 mL) lemon juice
8 oz (225 g) salmon fillet, chopped
½ cup (125 mL) diced onions
1 tsp (5 mL) chopped garlic
½ cup (125 mL) diced celery
1 tbsp (15 mL) chopped fresh parsley
1 tsp (5 mL) salt
½ tsp (2 mL) black pepper
For cooking:
2 tbsp (30 mL) butter
2 tbsp (30 mL) olive oil

In food processor or blender, liquefy hake with lemon juice. In large bowl, combine hake and lemon juice, salmon, onions, garlic, celery, parsley, salt and black pepper.

Form into patties and refrigerate until chilled.

In non-stick frying pan over medium heat, melt butter and heat oil. Sauté until golden brown on both sides, turning once.

4 fishcakes / 2 servings

Suggested sauce: Lemon Dill Mayo

Basic Mayonnaise *(author's recipe)*

1 egg yolk
2 tsp (10 mL) white vinegar
1 tsp (5 mL) dry mustard
7 oz (210 mL) canola oil
lemon juice
salt
pepper

Using blender, food processor or whip attachment of mixing bowl lets you make fast, easy homemade mayonnaise. It takes a little longer and a strong arm if done by hand, but the results will be worth the effort.

Whip egg yolk, vinegar and mustard. Add oil, drop by drop, whisking constantly until emulsion is formed. You will see mixture begin to thicken and turn pale. Continue adding oil slowly, adding lemon juice when sauce becomes thick.

Season with salt, pepper and lemon juice to taste.

Note: Ensure intact eggs (no cracks) are used to make mayonnaise.

Variations

Add to Basic Mayonnaise recipe for:

Curry Mango Mayo: 1 tbsp (15 mL) curry paste and ½ cup (125 mL) chopped mango, including juice.

Lemon Dill Mayo: fresh chopped dill and lemon juice to taste.

Smoked Salmon, Potato and Portobello Mushroom Cakes

Duncreigan Country Inn, Mabou Harbour, NS

"Scale the fish first!" when making fishcakes, advises chef Charles Mullendore.

1 cup (250 mL) mashed potatoes (½ lb/225 g/ about 5 medium peeled potatoes)
2 large portobello mushroom caps
1 tbsp (15 mL) olive oil
1 tsp (5 mL) butter
½ cup (125 mL) diced green onions
1 tbsp (15 mL) fresh chopped basil
1 tbsp (15 mL) fresh chopped thyme
1 tbsp (15 mL) fresh chopped parsley
1 tsp (5 mL) salt
1 tsp (5 mL) black pepper
8 oz (225 g) smoked salmon, diced
4 oz (110 g) Mabou cheese,* crumbled
½ cup (125 mL) spinach, cooked and chopped
For cooking:
butter

Peel and cube potatoes. In large pot, cover potatoes with cold water and bring to boil, cooking until easily pierced with knife. Drain and mash.

Brush mushroom caps with olive oil and grill 10 minutes. Chop and set aside.

In butter, sauté onions until soft. Stir in basil, thyme and parsley, set aside to cool.

In large bowl combine potatoes, smoked salmon, mushrooms, green onions, basil, thyme, parsley, salt, pepper, cheese and spinach.

Form into patties and refrigerate for several hours.

In large skillet, melt butter over medium heat. Sauté until golden brown on each side, turning once.

8 fishcakes / 4 servings

Suggested sauce: Red Pepper Aïoli

*Mabou cheese is a local delicacy. Substitute feta if you cannot get Mabou cheese.

Red Pepper Aïoli *(author's recipe)*

2 egg yolks
1 cup (250 mL) canola oil
1 roasted red pepper, peeled and seeded
1 ripe tomato, cored and seeded
1 clove garlic, minced
½ tsp (2 mL) lemon juice
salt and pepper to taste

In food processor, combine egg yolks and oil to the consistency of mayonnaise. Add red pepper, tomato, garlic and lemon juice. Pulse until smooth.

Season to taste with salt and pepper.

Store in refrigerator.

Salmon Cakes

Gabrieau's Bistro, Antigonish, NS

Chef Mark Gabrieau thinks of this as a down-home traditional fishcake. It's a very versatile recipe as one can substitute haddock or cod for salmon. He suggests combining the potato and salmon just enough to form a patty.

1 lb (455 g) salmon fillet
2 cups (500 mL) mashed potatoes (1 lb/455 g/ about 10 medium peeled potatoes)
¼ cup (50 mL) butter
1 tsp (5 mL) minced garlic
1 cup (250 mL) diced onions
½ cup (125 mL) chopped parsley or chives
1 tsp (5 mL) salt
½ tsp (2 mL) pepper
For cooking:
vegetable oil

Bring saucepan or deep skillet of water to boil; turn heat to medium and place salmon in pan, ensuring water covers fish. Cook until salmon flakes apart easily, drain and let cool.

Peel and cube potatoes. In large pot, cover potatoes with cold water and bring to boil, cooking until easily pierced with knife. Drain and mash.

Heat butter in frying pan over medium heat; add garlic and onions and cook, stirring frequently, until lightly browned.

Combine salmon, potatoes, garlic, onions, parsley or chives and salt and pepper in bowl. Form into patties and refrigerate overnight.

Heat oil in skillet over medium heat, add patties and fry until golden brown on one side, then flip and finish cooking on other side. Remove from pan, pat with paper towels and serve.

8 fishcakes / 4 servings

Suggested sauce: Pommery Mustard Cream

Pommery Mustard Cream *(author's recipe)*
1 cup (250 mL) whipping cream (35%)
1 tsp (5 mL) lemon juice
1 tbsp (15 mL) grainy mustard (Pommery)
salt and pepper to taste

Over medium heat in heavy-bottomed saucepan, simmer cream until reduced by one third. Stir in lemon juice and mustard. Remove from heat and serve, or refrigerate for later use.

Cornmeal-crusted Salmon Cakes

Windsor House, St. Andrews-by-the-Sea, NB

Chef Peter Woodworth says the combination of apricot almond chutney and salmon makes these cakes just right for brunch. He loves the freshness of green onions, especially combined with salmon, and adds that the seasoned crust has "a little bit of punch to it."

1 lb (455 g) salmon
4 tbsp (60 mL) thinly sliced green onions
1 egg, lightly beaten
½ tsp (2 mL) salt
¼ tsp (1 mL) pepper
For crust:
⅔ cup (175 mL) cornmeal
3 tsp (15 mL) cumin
1 tsp (5 mL) cayenne pepper
½ tsp (2 mL) cinnamon
2 tbsp (30 mL) fresh tarragon
For cooking:
olive oil

Bring saucepan or deep skillet of water to boil; turn heat to medium and place salmon in pan, ensuring water covers fish. Cook until salmon flakes apart easily, drain and let cool.

In large bowl combine salmon, green onions, egg, salt and pepper.

Form into patties. These will be crumbly, and very fragile. Refrigerate several hours or overnight to help keep shape when cooking.

In separate bowl, combine cornmeal, cumin, cayenne pepper, cinnamon and tarragon. Mix well.

Gently cover patties with crust mixture.

In a non-stick pan over medium heat, heat olive oil and sauté until golden brown, turning very carefully only once.

4 fishcakes / 2 servings

Suggested sauce: Apricot Almond Chutney

Apricot Almond Chutney

1 cup (250 mL) sliced sundried apricots
4 shallots, diced
2 cloves garlic, smashed
3 tbsp (45 mL) olive oil
1 ½ cups (350 mL) white wine
½ cup (125 mL) honey
¾ cup (175 mL) white wine vinegar

Combine ingredients in medium size pot, on medium-high heat. Bring to boil then let simmer on medium heat for about 8 to 10 minutes. Let cool.

Salmon Cakes

Sweet Basil Bistro, Halifax, NS

Chef Veinotte serves his salmon cakes with any one of three sauces: his original curry cream sauce, a caper sauce or with dill cucumber sauce.

1 cup (250 mL) mashed potatoes (½ lb/225 g/ about 5 medium peeled potatoes)
6 oz (170 g) salmon fillets
2 tbsp (30 mL) chopped fresh cilantro
1 tsp (5 mL) minced chives
¼ tsp (1 mL) Tabasco sauce
¼ tsp (1 mL) Worcestershire sauce
1 egg
2 tbsp (30 mL) mayonnaise
¼ tsp (1 mL) black pepper
½ tsp (2 mL) salt
For breading:
2 cups (500 mL) plain white fresh breadcrumbs
For cooking:
butter

Peel and cube potatoes. In large pot, cover potatoes with cold water and bring to boil, cooking until easily pierced with knife. Drain and mash.

Bring saucepan or deep skillet of water to a boil; turn heat to medium and place salmon in pan, ensuring water covers fish. Cook until salmon flakes apart easily, drain and let cool.

In large bowl, combine potatoes, salmon, cilantro, chives, Tabasco sauce, Worcestershire sauce, egg, mayonnaise, salt and pepper.

Form into patties.

Roll in breadcrumbs to coat thoroughly.

In a non-stick frying pan, heat butter and fry over medium-high heat until golden brown.

4 fishcakes / 2 servings

Suggested sauce: Curry Cream Sauce

Curry Cream Sauce *(author's recipe)*

To one recipe of Béchamel (below), whisk in
1-2 tbsp (5-10 mL) mild curry paste
¼ cup (50 mL) lemon juice
OR:
1 cup (250 mL) whipping cream (35%)
1-2 tsp (5-10 mL) mild curry paste
1 tsp (5 mL) lemon juice

Over medium heat in heavy-bottomed saucepan, simmer cream (if using) until reduced by one third. Stir in curry paste and lemon juice. Remove from heat and serve, or refrigerate for later use.

Béchamel Sauce (author's recipe)

4 oz (115 g) clarified butter*
4 oz (115 g) flour
4 cups (2 L) milk, hot
1 small whole onion, peeled
1 whole clove
1 small bay leaf
salt
white pepper
nutmeg

The classic white sauce, béchamel is versatile and can take on many different seasonings.

Heat butter in heavy saucepan over low heat. Add flour, stirring to make roux. Gradually add milk, whisking constantly.

Bring sauce to boil, whisking, then reduce heat to simmer.

Stick bay leaf to onion with clove and add to sauce.

Simmer for 30 minutes, stirring occasionally.

Season very lightly with salt, white pepper and nutmeg.

Strain to remove onion.

Sauce may be made immediately, or refrigerated and reheated for later use.

*To clarify butter, heat unsalted butter slowly in heavy saucepan. The milk solids will separate and sink to the bottom. Skim foam off top, carefully pour off the liquid, which is your clarified butter (also known as drawn butter), and discard the solids. Because the milk solid has been removed, clarified butter can be heated to a higher temperature before burning, making it ideal for pan-frying. Using 2 ½ lbs (1 kg) of butter will yield 2 lbs (910 g) clarified butter.

Salmon and Broccoli Fishcakes

Gaffer's Bistro, Whitehall Country Inn,
Clarenville, NFLD

This recipe started out as salmon cakes served with a cheese sauce, but Chef Chris Sheppard feels it is much improved by mixing the cheddar into the patty mixture.

5 oz (145 g) salmon, boneless, skinless fillet
2 cups (500 mL) mashed potatoes (1 lb/455 g/
   about 10 medium peeled potatoes)
½ cup (125 mL) broccoli florets, cut small
¼ cup (50 mL) grated cheddar cheese
1 tsp (5 mL) salt
1 tsp (5 mL) white pepper
For cooking:
butter

Bring saucepan or deep skillet of water to boil; turn heat to medium and place salmon in pan, ensuring water covers fish. Cook until salmon flakes apart easily. Drain and let cool.

Peel and cube potatoes. In large pot, cover potatoes with cold water and bring to boil, cooking until easily pierced with knife. Drain and mash.

Bring pot of water to boil, plunge broccoli in for about 5 seconds, remove from water and immediately put broccoli into bowl of ice water. Cool and drain well.*

In large bowl, combine salmon, potatoes, broccoli, cheese, salt and pepper.

Form into patties.

In a non-stick skillet, melt butter over medium heat until it begins to foam. Lightly brown patties on each side. Transfer patties to baking sheet and finish cooking in 400°F (200°C) oven for 10 to 12 minutes.

6 fishcakes / 3 servings

Suggested sauce: Lemon Herb Butter Sauce (see page 78)

*This is called blanching, and it helps set the colour of vegetables, as well as take away the raw taste.

Lobster

With today's lobster prices, it's hard to believe that in many fishing communities lobster was once considered a poor man's food. When buying live lobster, hold your choice out of the water; the tail should flap or curl under the body and not dangle listlessly. The quickest way to cook lobster is by plunging it headfirst into heavily-salted boiling water. If this doesn't appeal to you, ask your fish purveyor to cook it for you. Atlantic lobster can be found on the West Coast but at exorbitant prices; crab may be used in place of lobster with equally good results in these recipes.

Chipotle Lime Lobster Cakes

Garrison House Inn, Annapolis Royal, NS

Chipotle peppers were traditionally smoked in clay pots in a fire pit. Modern methods of curing the peppers gives them a fuller, mellower flavour that rounds out the palate rather than shocking the taste buds with a sudden heat.

1 lb (455 g) lobster meat
1 egg
1 tbsp (15 mL) lime juice
1 tsp (5 mL) chipotle peppers*
1 cup (250 mL) fresh breadcrumbs
1 tsp (5 mL) garlic powder
2 tbsp (30 mL) mayonnaise
1 tsp (5 mL) chopped fresh cilantro
For cooking:
olive oil

In large bowl, combine all ingredients.

Form into patties.

In large skillet, heat oil over medium heat. Sauté until golden brown on each side, turning once.

4 fishcakes / 2 servings

Suggested sauce: Cucumber Raita

*Chipotles are dried, smoked jalapenos. They can be usually be found in the Mexican food section. Substitute chili paste if unavailable. When mincing chipotles or any hot peppers, wear gloves and remove seeds and membrane carefully before chopping – the seeds contain most of the "heat." Contact with the bare skin can result in painful burning.

Cucumber Raita (author's recipe)
1 English cucumber
½ cup (125 mL) plain yogurt
1 tsp (5 mL) chopped fresh mint

Peel and seed cucumber. Dice into small cubes. In bowl, mix cucumber, yogurt and mint. Serve chilled.

Chilled Lobster Salad Cakes

Le Crocodile, Vancouver, BC

This very light lobster cake should gently fall apart at the touch of a fork. By cooking the potatoes with the skins on, enough starch is retained to allow the cakes to hold their shape. Be sure to use red potatoes.

1 lb (455 g) red-skinned potatoes (about 10 medium potatoes)
8 stalks young asparagus
12 red radishes
1 tbsp (15 mL) finely chopped onions
8 oz (225 g) lobster meat
½ tsp (2 mL) salt
¼ tsp (1 mL) pepper
1 tbsp (15 mL) lemon juice
2 tbsp (30 mL) Dijon mustard vinaigrette* (or other vinaigrette)

Boil potatoes until easily pierced with knife. Set aside to cool.

Slice into quarters and carefully mince.

Cook asparagus in boiling water, cool in ice water. Slice thinly.

Slice radishes thinly.

In mixing bowl, combine potatoes, asparagus, radishes, onions, lobster, salt, pepper and lemon juice. Toss in vinaigrette.

Mold in small plastic or metal rings, let chill and unmold.

4 fishcakes / 2 servings

*Dijon Mustard Vinaigrette (1 part oil to 3 parts vinegar, 1 tsp Dijon mustard or more to taste) or use the vinaigrette of your choice.

Lobster Croquettes

Opa!, Halifax, NS

Chef Joseph says these lobster croquettes were inspired by another favourite served at the restaurant, a dish of chicken stuffed with lobster, scallops and shrimps, using lime zest and juice, and finished with a rich wine cream sauce. He adds that citrus zest adds a lot to almost any dish.

2 cups (500 mL) mashed potatoes (1 lb/455 g/ about 10 medium peeled potatoes)
¼ cup (50 mL) butter
1 cup (250 mL) diced onions
12 oz (340 g) lobster meat
12 oz (340 g) baby shrimp
1 tsp (5 mL) orange zest
1 tsp (5 mL) orange juice
1 tsp (5 mL) fresh chopped thyme
3 tsp (15 mL) fresh chopped parsley
2 egg yolks

¼ cup (50 mL) fresh breadcrumbs
¼ tsp (1 mL) black pepper
½ tsp (2 mL) salt
For breading:
2 eggs, beaten
1 cup (250 mL) flour
2 cups (500 mL) fresh breadcrumbs
For cooking:
vegetable oil

Peel and cube potatoes. In a large pot, cover potatoes with cold water and bring to boil, cooking until easily pierced with knife. Drain and mash.

Melt butter in frying pan and sauté onions until softened but not browned.

In large bowl, combine mashed potatoes, onions (with butter), lobster meat, baby shrimp, orange zest and juice, thyme, parsley, egg yolks, ¼ cup (50 mL) breadcrumbs, salt and pepper.

Mix thoroughly. Form into patties.

Set up breading station: 3 bowls left to right, first flour, then egg mixture, then breadcrumbs. Dip patties in flour, shake off excess; dip in egg mixture then coat in 2 cups (500 mL) breadcrumbs.

Cook in vegetable oil until brown and serve.

5 fishcakes / 2-3 servings

Suggested sauce: Béarnaise Sauce

Béarnaise Sauce (author's recipe)
½ cup (125 mL) white wine vinegar
2 tbsp (30 mL) chopped shallots
2 tsp (10 mL) chopped fresh tarragon
1 tsp (5 mL) pepper
6 egg yolks
1 lb (455 g) warm clarified butter (see page 17)
lemon juice
salt

Combine vinegar, shallots, tarragon and pepper in saucepan and reduce by ¾. Remove from heat and allow to cool slightly.

Transfer to stainless steel bowl.

Add egg yolks to bowl and beat well using wire whisk.

Hold bowl over a hot water bath (double boiler) and continue to beat yolks until thick and creamy.

Remove bowl from heat. Slowly and gradually beat in warm, clarified butter, adding drop by drop at first.

If the sauce becomes too thick, beat in a little lemon juice.

When all butter has been added, taste.

Add more salt and pepper if you like.

Serve immediately.

Shrimp & Scallops

Enormously popular and versatile, shrimp is harvested on both east and west coasts. Jumbo shrimp are commonly called "prawns" on the west coast, although this is a misnomer as the prawn is actually a separate species. The smaller, colder water species tend to be the sweetest and most flavourful. Shrimp is widely available fresh, frozen and canned; cooked and uncooked; shell on and shell off — take your pick. While there are slight differences in taste and texture, all sizes work well for fishcakes.

Scallops are generally grouped in two classes: the tiny bay scallop and the larger sea scallop. As they deteriorate rapidly once harvested, it's rare to see fresh scallops in their shells. Look for creamy or pinkish-tinged flesh that is shiny and has a sweet odour.

Asian Seafood Cakes

Dundee Arms Inn, Charlottetown, PEI

Chef Patrick Young prepared this recipe with good health in mind: this mixture of seafood has a high content of Omega 3 fatty acids. He has been experimenting with Asian influences in his cuisine for many years.

2 oz (55 g) scallops
2 oz (55 g) shrimp
2 oz (55 g) haddock
2 oz (55 g) salmon
1 cup (250 mL) mashed potatoes (½ lb/225 g/ about 5 medium peeled potatoes)
1 cup (250 mL) cooked Japanese white rice* (short grain or sticky)
¼ cup (50 mL) diced carrots
¼ cup (50 mL) diced bell peppers (red, green or yellow or combination)
¼ cup (50 mL) diced red onions
¼ tsp (1 mL) diced garlic
¼ tsp (1 mL) diced shallots
1 tsp (5 mL) white sesame seeds
1 tsp (5 mL) black sesame seeds
⅛ cup (25 mL) sesame oil
¼ cup (50 mL) soy sauce
1 egg
2 tsp (125 mL) fresh breadcrumbs
For cooking:
vegetable oil

*If you have trouble locating the short grain or sticky Japanese rice, Arborio, the Italian short grain rice, may be used.

Dice or chop seafood into small pieces. Bring pot of water to simmer, place fish in pot and cook until done. Cool and set aside.

Peel and cube potatoes. In large pot, cover potatoes with cold water and bring to boil, cooking until easily pierced with knife. Drain and mash.

In large bowl, combine seafood, potatoes, rice, carrots, peppers, red onions, garlic, shallots, black and white sesame seeds, sesame oil, soy sauce, egg and breadcrumbs.

The mixture will be fairly wet. Form into patties.

Pan-fry in vegetable oil over medium-high heat, 4 to 5 minutes each side.

7 fishcakes / 3-4 servings

Suggested sauce: Wasabi Cream Sauce

Wasabi Cream Sauce
1 tbsp (15 mL) butter
¼ tsp (1 mL) minced shallots
¼ tsp (1 mL) minced garlic
½ cup (125 mL) dry white wine
2 cups (500 mL) whipping cream (35%)
1 tsp (5 mL) wasabi powder

In frying pan over medium heat, sauté shallots and garlic in butter until browning starts. Add white wine, stirring with whisk, and cook a few minutes until wine has almost evaporated. Add cream and cook, stirring occasionally, until sauce begins to thicken.

Stir in wasabi powder and serve.

Shrimp Cakes

Halliburton House Inn, Halifax, NS

Chef Scott describes this as a "special occasion dish" that he introduced for Valentine's Day a few years ago. The recipe began as a more traditional cake using a potato binder and finished as an intensely flavourful dish designed to give the seafood centre stage.

Mousse:
4 oz (115 g) scallops
¼ cup (50 mL) butter, softened
1 tbsp (15 mL) lime juice
½ cup (125 mL) heavy cream (35%)
1 egg white
Patties:
8 oz (225 g) deveined shrimp (large, raw, peeled, coarsely chopped)
2 tbsp (30 mL) chopped green onions
¼ cup (50 mL) chopped cilantro
1 tbsp (15 mL) Asian red chili paste
1 tsp (5 mL) lime juice
1 tsp (5 mL) salt
½ tsp (2 mL) pepper
For breading:
1 cup (250 mL) panko breadcrumbs*
For cooking:
vegetable oil

In food processor or blender, purée scallops, butter, lime juice, cream and egg white until smooth.

Combine shrimp, green onions, cilantro, chili paste, lime juice, salt and pepper in bowl; fold in mousse mixture. Form into patties; mixture should be just thick enough to hold its shape. Refrigerate formed patties for several hours.

Preheat oven to 400°F (200°C). Heat oil in ovenproof skillet. Roll patties in breadcrumbs and cook in oil over medium heat until lightly browned, then place skillet in oven for 8 to 10 minutes until shrimp cakes are cooked through.

4 fishcakes / 2 servings

Suggested sauce: Maltaise Sauce

*Panko breadcrumbs, also known as Japanese-style breadcrumbs, are larger, flakier and lighter than traditional breadcrumbs.

Maltaise Sauce (author's recipe)
¼ tsp (1 mL) salt
¼ tsp (1 mL) pepper
1 ½ oz (45 mL) white vinegar (or white wine vinegar)
1 oz (30 mL) cold water
6 egg yolks
2-4 oz (60-120 mL) orange juice
1 lb (455 g) warm clarified butter (see page 17)

Maltaise is hollandaise with orange juice (classically, juice from blood oranges) added.

Combine salt, pepper and vinegar in saucepan and reduce until nearly dry. Remove from heat and add cold water.

Transfer to stainless steel bowl. Add egg yolks to bowl and beat well using wire whisk. Hold bowl over hot water bath (double boiler) and continue to beat yolks until thick and creamy.

Remove bowl from heat. Slowly and gradually beat in warm, clarified butter, adding butter drop by drop at first. If sauce becomes too thick, beat in a little orange juice. When all butter has been added, add remaining orange juice. Taste and add more salt and pepper if you like. Serve immediately.

West Coast Fishcakes

The Teahouse Restaurant, Vancouver, BC

Chef Lynda Larouche uses a combination of fresh seafood that is readily available. This could be an appetizer or a main course.

2 cups (500 mL) peeled and diced red potatoes
   (1 lb/500 g/about 10 medium peeled
   potatoes)
1 cup (250 mL) minced onion
1 tsp (5 mL) vegetable oil
8 oz (225 mL) cooked shrimp
8 oz (225 mL) cooked salmon
8 oz (225 mL) cooked cod
1 cup (250 mL) mayonnaise
2 tsp (10 mL) chopped fresh parsley
1 tbsp (15 mL) roasted chopped garlic
salt and pepper to taste
For breading:
1 cup (250 mL) fresh breadcrumbs
For cooking:
vegetable oil

Place potatoes in large pot of cold water and bring to boil. Drain and set aside.

Sauté onions in oil until tender but not browned, set aside.

Bring saucepan or deep skillet of water to a boil; turn heat to medium and place cod and haddock in pan, ensuring water covers fish. Cook until well done and flakes apart easily. Set aside to cool.

In large bowl, combine shrimp, salmon, cod, mayonnaise, parsley, garlic, potatoes and onions. Season with salt and pepper to taste.

Form into patties, coat with breadcrumbs.

Sauté over medium heat in oil until browned on both sides, turning once.

6 fishcakes / 3 servings

Suggested Sauce: Apple Vinaigrette with Basil Leaves

Apple Vinaigrette with Basil Leaves
2 Granny Smith apples, peeled and cored
2 tbsp (30 mL) minced shallots
1 tbsp (15 mL) minced ginger root
½ cup (125 mL) mirin*
½ cup (125 mL) rice vinegar
⅓ cup (75 mL) soy sauce
salt and pepper to taste
10 basil leaves

Place apples, shallots, ginger, mirin, rice vinegar and soy sauce in blender and process until smooth. Add salt and pepper to taste.

Toss basil leaves in vinaigrette and serve with fishcakes.

*If you do not have mirin, substitute apple cider vinegar.

Crab

There are several species of crabs referred to in these recipes, from the East Coast's Snow or Queen crab to the Dungeness and King crabs on the Pacific side. All crab types may be used interchangeably in crab cake recipes, so go with whatever's fresh and in season.

When buying live crab, look for active specimens and avoid those that appear sluggish or aren't moving. If you're squeamish about throwing live crustaceans in the cooking pot, ask your fish purveyor to do it for you. For convenience, there is high quality, shelled, frozen product available year-round. When buying lump crab meat, pick through it carefully for shell fragments.

Thai Spiced Crab Cakes

Arbor View Inn, Lunenburg, NS

Chef Daniel Orovec says, "The lighter, more exotic flavour in the crab cake comes from using Japanese breadcrumbs instead of potatoes. You can vary the recipe with Thai curry, cilantro and green onions to enhance the oriental flavour. It can also be served with a mango salsa."

1 lb (455 g) crab meat, drained
½ cup (125 mL) finely diced red peppers
¼ cup (50 mL) finely diced red onions
4 tsp (20 mL) finely chopped green onions
2 tsp (10 mL) Thai chili sauce
salt and pepper to taste
½ cup (125 mL) mayonnaise
1 cup (250 mL) panko breadcrumbs
For cooking:
2 tbsp (30 mL) vegetable oil
2 tbsp (30 mL) butter

Combine crab, red pepper, red and green onions, Thai chili sauce, salt and pepper in large bowl. Mix in mayonnaise, then fold in breadcrumbs until well mixed. Form into patties and refrigerate for at least 1 hour.

Heat a non-stick pan, add vegetable oil and butter and heat until butter is sizzling.

Sauté until golden brown on both sides.

6 fishcakes / 3 servings

Suggested sauce: Pear Chutney

Pear Chutney

1 tbsp (15 mL) vegetable oil
1 diced medium onion
3 peeled, cored and diced medium pears
6 tbsp (90 mL) packed golden brown sugar
⅓ cup (75 mL) golden raisins
3 tbsp (45 mL) apple cider vinegar
2 tbsp (30 mL) fresh lemon juice
1 tbsp (15 mL) chopped fresh ginger
4 whole cloves

Heat oil in heavy-bottomed saucepan over medium heat. Add onions, sauté until tender.

Add pears, sugar, raisins, vinegar, lemon juice, ginger and cloves and bring to boil.

Reduce heat and simmer, uncovered, for about 20 minutes or until pears are tender. Remove cloves.

Chill and serve.

Crab Cakes de Bouctouche

Auberge Le Vieux Presbytère Restaurant,
Bouctouche, NB

Baking powder gives a lightness to this moist cake.

1 lb (455 g) crab meat, drained
1 cup (250 mL) fresh breadcrumbs
⅓ cup (75 mL) milk
¼ cup (50 mL) mayonnaise
1 egg
2 tbsp (30 mL) finely chopped green onions
1 tbsp (15 mL) chopped fresh parsley
½ tsp (2 mL) baking powder
½ tsp (2 mL) salt
¼ tsp (1 mL) white pepper
For cooking:
2 tbsp (30 mL) vegetable oil
2 tbsp (30 mL) butter
flour

Place crab meat in large bowl. Cover with breadcrumbs and pour milk on top. In a separate bowl, combine mayonnaise, egg, green onions, parsley, baking powder, salt and pepper. Pour over crab mixture and gently toss until mixed.

Form into patties and refrigerate for at least 1 hour.

Heat butter with oil in large skillet over medium heat.

Dust cakes lightly with flour and fry until golden brown, about 4 minutes each side.

4 fishcakes / 2 servings

Suggested sauce: Lemon Herb Butter Sauce (see page 78)

Crab Cakes

Eagle's Eye Restaurant, Golden, BC

This recipe calls for any white fish. Chef Dave Knoop's first choice is halibut, which complements the crab and offers a light, flaky texture to the dish. Other alternatives include monkfish and jackfish, which have a mild flavour.

7 oz (200 g) cod, haddock or halibut, cooked
  (or other white fish)
11 oz (300 g) crab meat
2 eggs
1 tbsp (15 mL) fresh dill
½ tsp (2 mL) salt
¼ tsp (1 mL) pepper
1 tbsp (15 mL) fresh lemon juice
fresh breadcrumbs

Bring saucepan or deep skillet of water to boil; turn heat to medium and place fish in pan, ensuring water completely covers it. Cook until well done and flakes apart easily. Remove any bones. Combine fish with all other ingredients.

Form into patties, adding breadcrumbs if mixture is too moist.

Sauté in butter until brown on both sides, turning once.

6 fishcakes / 3 servings

Suggested sauce: Pommery Mustard Cream (see page 14)

Dungeness Crab Cakes

Country Squire, Naramata, BC

Owner Patt Dyck likes to showcase Dungeness crab with only a little seasoning. They are best served hot with a very cold sauce. She suggests strawberry relish and a dollop of black pepper mayonnaise.

2 lb (900 g) Dungeness crab meat
2 cups (500 mL) black pepper mayonnaise
2 large egg whites
¼ cup (50 mL) crushed saltine crackers
¼ tsp (1 mL) Tabasco sauce
salt and pepper to taste
For breading:
2 cups (500 mL) fine breadcrumbs
For cooking:
canola oil

In large mixing bowl, combine crab, mayonnaise, egg whites, cracker crumbs and Tabasco sauce. Add salt and pepper to taste.

Form into patties and refrigerate until chilled. Roll in breadcrumbs to coat.

Fry in oil over medium heat until golden brown on both sides, turning once.

10 fishcakes / 5 servings

Black Pepper Mayonnaise

2 eggs
½ tsp (2 mL) dry mustard
½ tsp (2 mL) salt
1 tbsp (15 mL) lemon juice
1 tbsp (15 mL) white wine vinegar
2 cups (500 mL) canola oil
2-3 shallots, minced
1 tbsp (15 mL) freshly ground black pepper
2-4 drops Tabasco sauce

Put eggs, mustard and salt into food processor and process 30 seconds. Add lemon juice and vinegar and process. Very slowly add oil with processor running. Add shallots, black pepper and Tabasco sauce, process for 2 to 3 minutes. Refrigerate until ready to use.

Note: Ensure intact eggs (no cracks) are used to make any uncooked mayonnaise.

Country Squire Strawberry Relish

¼ cup (50 mL) red wine vinegar
¼ cup (50 mL) orange juice
2 tbsp (30 mL) finely minced fresh ginger
3 cups (750 mL) finely diced fresh strawberries
1-2 tbsp (15-30 mL) honey

Combine vinegar, orange juice and ginger in saucepan. Bring to boil, then reduce heat and simmer 3 to 5 minutes. Add strawberries and continue simmering for 10 minutes. Cool, and stir in honey.

Bay of Fundy Cakes

Dufferin Inn, Saint John, NB

Chef Axel Begner developed this recipe to reflect the inn's location on the shores of the Bay of Fundy. He uses very fresh shellfish — lobster, crab and scallops — and sometimes salmon. His partner Margaret says the cakes should be prepared and served the same day otherwise they will not hold their shape.

½ lb (225 g) crab meat
½ lb (225 g) lobster meat
½ lb (225 g) scallops
4 tbsp (60 mL) chopped green onions
2 tsp (10 mL) diced shallots
2 tsp (10 mL) diced garlic
1 tbsp (15 mL) chopped fresh dill
1 tbsp (15 mL) chopped fresh parsley
2 tbsp (30 mL) chopped capers
¼ cup (50 mL) mayonnaise
1 tsp (5 mL) salt
⅓ tsp (2 mL) pepper
3 tbsp (45 mL) fresh breadcrumbs
1 tbsp (15 mL) lemon juice
4 egg yolks
For cooking:
olive oil

In large bowl, combine all ingredients, except olive oil. Form into patties.

Heat olive oil in skillet over medium-high heat. Brown patties on both sides, then place in 350°F (180°C) oven for 15 minutes until heated through.

7 fishcakes / 3-4 servings

Suggested sauce: Moosehead Beer Sauce

Moosehead Beer Sauce
6 egg yolks
1 bottle Moosehead Dry beer (or other dry ale)
1 tbsp (15 mL) maple syrup
¼ tsp (1 mL) salt
¼ tsp (1 mL) pepper
1 tbsp (15 mL) lemon juice

In large stainless steel bowl, whisk together egg yolks, beer, maple syrup, salt, pepper and lemon juice. Sit bowl over pot of boiling water and keep whisking until sauce is thick and creamy.

Chef Richard Boulier's Crab Cakes

Hatfield Heritage Inn, Hartland, NB

Chef Richard Boulier says he likes to base his recipes around an accentuating ingredient such as Dijon mustard, balsamic vinegar or, as in this case, green onions. He says he has to carefully watch the balance of the ingredients.

½ cup (125 mL) mashed potatoes (¼ lb/115 g/ about 2 large peeled potatoes)
1 lb (455 g) crab meat
1 cup (250 mL) breadcrumbs
1 tbsp (15 mL) chopped parsley
8 tsp (5 mL) finely chopped green onions
1 egg white
4 tsp (20 mL) lemon juice
½ tsp (2 mL) dry mustard
½ tsp (2 mL) paprika
½ tsp (2 mL) salt
¼ tsp (1 mL) black pepper
For breading:
½ cup (125 mL) skim milk
1 egg white
½ cup (125 mL) breadcrumbs
For cooking:
4 tbsp (60 mL) butter
2 tbsp (30 mL) vegetable oil

Peel and cube potatoes. In large pot, cover potatoes with cold water and bring to boil, cooking until easily pierced with knife. Drain and mash.

In large bowl, combine potatoes, crab, breadcrumbs, parsley, green onions, 1 egg white, lemon juice, mustard, paprika, salt and pepper.

Form into patties and refrigerate several hours or overnight.

Whisk other egg white and milk in small bowl. Dip patties into milk, then coat with breadcrumbs.

In heavy skillet, heat butter and vegetable oil.

Add crab cakes, cooking until both sides are golden brown.

5 fishcakes / 2-3 servings

Suggested sauce: Lemon Dill Cream Sauce

Lemon Dill Cream Sauce
1 cup (250 mL) Béchamel sauce (see page 17)
¼ cup (50 mL) chopped fresh dill
¼ cup (50mL) lemon juice

Stir dill and lemon juice into Béchamel and serve.

Dungeness Crab Cakes

Catch Restaurant, Calgary, AB

Chef Andrew Hewson advises that you should use just enough of the scallop mousse to bind the cakes. Any extra scallop mousse can be rolled in plastic wrap (like a cigar) and poached. It can be used as a garnish or as an hors d'oeuvre topping.

Mousse:
3 oz (80 g) scallops
pinch salt and pepper
1 egg yolk
3 tbsp (45 mL) whipping cream (35%)

Patties:
1 tbsp (15 mL) butter
1 tbsp (15 mL) finely diced onions
1 tbsp (15 mL) finely diced leeks
1 tbsp (15 mL) finely diced fennel
2 tbsp (30 mL) finely diced red pepper
1 lb (455 g) Dungeness crab meat
1 tbsp (15 mL) chopped parsley
2 tsp (10 mL) chopped cilantro
½ tsp (2 mL) salt
½ tsp (2 mL) paprika
¼ tsp (1 mL) pepper
¼ tsp (1 mL) cayenne pepper

For breading:

1 cup (250 mL) panko breadcrumbs

1 tsp (5 mL) finely chopped orange zest

1 tsp (5 mL) finely chopped lemon zest

1 tsp (5 mL) finely chopped lime zest

1 tsp (5 mL) chopped fresh parsley

For cooking:

vegetable oil

Prepare scallop mousse: in food processor, purée scallops with a pinch of salt and a shake of pepper. Scrape down sides of bowl and add egg yolk, puréeing 30 seconds. Scrape down sides of bowl. With processor running, slowly pour in cream. Refrigerate mousse until ready to use.

In skillet over medium heat, melt butter and gently cook onions, leeks, fennel and red peppers until vegetables are tender but not browned. Set aside to cool.

In large mixing bowl, combine cooled vegetables with crab meat, parsley, cilantro, salt, paprika, pepper, and cayenne pepper. Form into patties and refrigerate until chilled.

In small bowl, combine panko breadcrumbs, orange, lemon and lime zest and parsley.

Coat patties with breading mixture.

Sauté in vegetable oil over medium-high heat until golden brown on both sides, turning once.

4 fishcakes / 2 servings

Suggested sauce: Mango Chutney

Mango Chutney

7 tbsp (100 mL) rice wine vinegar

⅓ cup (80 mL) sugar

4 tsp (20 mL) ginger, peeled and chopped fine

2 tsp (10 mL) shallot, chopped fine

1 tsp (5 mL) mustard seed

1 ripe mango, peeled and diced

1 tsp (5 mL) cilantro, chopped

In a small pot, combine rice wine vinegar, sugar, ginger, shallot and mustard seed and reduce to syrup consistency.

Add mango and cook 3 to 5 minutes, strain liquid from mango and return to pot to reduce back down to syrup.

Add mango back to the syrup and let cool, stir in cilantro and keep in fridge until ready to use. Chutney will last 2 weeks.

Dungeness Crab Cakes

Mahle House, Nanaimo, BC

Chef Maureen Loucks makes stunning seafood towers for her unsuspecting guests. First splash a little scallion oil and red pepper purée on the plate. "Throw it down on the plate and it splatters wildly," she advises. Then place a dab of the aïoli sauce on the plate followed by the crab cake. Then add another dab of aïoli to the top of the cake and place a grilled scallop to top it all off, with two tiger prawns on the side.

1 tsp (5 mL) butter
1 cup (250 mL) finely diced red peppers
1 ½ lb (675 g) fresh Dungeness crab meat
1 tbsp (15 mL) fresh chopped chives
½ cup (125 mL) panko breadcrumbs
½ cup (125 mL) mayonnaise
For breading:
1 cup (250 mL) panko breadcrumbs
3 eggs
For cooking:
butter
vegetable oil

Heat butter and cook red pepper gently until softened. Set aside and let cool.

In large bowl, combine crab, chives, red peppers, ½ cup (125 mL) breadcrumbs and mayonnaise.

Form into patties and refrigerate at least 1 hour or overnight.

In small bowl, whisk eggs. Dip patties in egg, then in 1 cup (250 mL) breadcrumbs.

In non-stick pan over medium-high heat, melt butter and add oil. Sauté until golden brown on both sides, turning once.

6 fishcakes / 3 servings

Suggested sauce: Saffron Aïoli

Saffron Aïoli (author's recipe)
3 or 4 saffron strands
¼ cup (50 mL) dry white wine
2 egg yolks
1 cup (250 mL) canola oil
1 clove garlic, minced
salt and pepper to taste

Soak saffron strands in wine to bring out colour.

Form emulsion with egg yolks and oil. Whisk eggs in small bowl. Add oil drop by drop, gradually increasing flow to thin stream until mixture thickens.

Add garlic, wine-saffron mix and season to taste.

Crab Cakes

Parker House Inn, Saint John, NB

This gluten-free recipe is a healthy choice, Chef Kathy Golding says, for anyone, not just those who suffer from allergies. Other fish, such as halibut, lobster or salmon, can be substituted for crab. This popular recipe is served with spicy tomato chutney at the inn.

1 cup (250 mL) mashed potatoes (½ lb/225 g/
  about 5 medium peeled potatoes)
1 tbsp (15 mL) olive oil
1 finely diced small onion
½ cup (125 mL) finely diced red pepper
8 oz (225 g) crab meat, drained
2 eggs, lightly beaten
salt and pepper to taste
For cooking:
canola oil

Peel and cube potatoes. In large pot, cover potatoes with cold water and bring to boil, cooking until easily pierced with knife. Drain and mash.

In skillet, heat olive oil and cook onions and red pepper until softened but not brown. Combine crab, eggs, onion, red pepper and potatoes, salt and pepper to taste, and form into patties.

Pan-fry in hot oil until golden brown on both sides.

6 fishcakes / 3 servings

Crab Cakes

Rim Rock Café, Whistler, BC

Chef Rolf Gunther presents these cakes by placing one cake on top of another, wrapping a slice of cucumber marinated in Japanese rice wine around the edges, and topping them with flying fish roe and shredded daikon radish. The bright orange roe contrasting with the cool green of the cucumber creates an inviting plate for hungry eyes.

1 lb (455 g) cooked crab meat, drained
⅓ cup (75 mL) finely diced red pepper
⅓ cup (75 mL) finely diced green pepper
⅓ cup (75 mL) finely diced yellow pepper
¼ cup (50 mL) finely minced shallots
¼ cup (50 mL) finely minced jalapeños (see
   page 22)
2 eggs, lightly beaten
2 tsp (10 mL) puréed roasted garlic*
1 cup (250 mL) fresh breadcrumbs
salt and pepper to taste

Combine crab meat, peppers, shallots, jalapeños, eggs, roasted garlic, breadcrumbs, salt and pepper. Form into patties and refrigerate for at least 1 hour.

Pan-fry in hot oil until golden brown on both sides.

7 fishcakes / 3-4 servings

Suggested sauce: Cucumber Raita (see page 22)

*Roasted garlic has a mellower flavour than raw garlic, with a smooth buttery texture. To roast garlic, drizzle head of garlic with olive oil, wrap in foil and roast in 350°F (180°C) oven until very soft. Makes an excellent spread.

Cornmeal-crusted Crab Cakes

Seasons Restaurant, Vancouver, BC

These crab cakes make a great lunch with the rémoulade and a few mixed greens. For another version of the dish, try panko (Japanese bread crumbs) instead of cornmeal and change the sauce to a lime ginger aïoli with a small amount of soya and sesame oil.

½ lb (225 g) crab meat
¼ cup (50 mL) very finely diced red pepper
¼ cup (50 mL) very finely diced celery
¼ cup (50 mL) very finely diced red onion
3 tbsp (45 mL) diced chives
1 cup (250 mL) fine breadcrumbs
1 cup (250 mL) mayonnaise

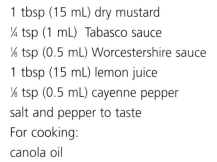

1 tbsp (15 mL) dry mustard
¼ tsp (1 mL) Tabasco sauce
⅛ tsp (0.5 mL) Worcestershire sauce
1 tbsp (15 mL) lemon juice
⅛ tsp (0.5 mL) cayenne pepper
salt and pepper to taste
For cooking:
canola oil

In large bowl, combine crab, red pepper, celery, onion, chives and breadcrumbs.

In second bowl, stir together mayonnaise, mustard, Tabasco sauce, Worcestershire sauce, lemon juice, cayenne, salt and pepper.

Fold crab mixture into seasoned mayonnaise. Form into patties and refrigerate until chilled.

Sauté over medium-high heat until browned on both sides, turning once.

4 fishcakes / 2 servings

Suggested sauce: Cajun Rémoulade (see page 57)

Potato Crab Cakes

Shaw's Hotel, Brackley Beach, PEI

The combination of diced celery, red pepper and parsley create a very colourful crab cake. The rich flavour comes from adding sour cream.

2 cups (500 mL) mashed potatoes (1 lb/455 g/ about 10 medium peeled potatoes)
2 tbsp (30 mL) butter
1 cup (250 mL) finely chopped Spanish onions
½ cup (125 mL) finely chopped celery
¼ cup (50 mL) finely chopped red bell pepper
1 tbsp (15 mL) chopped garlic
1 lb (455 g) crab meat
¼ cup (50 mL) chopped green onions (green part only)
¼ cup (50 mL) grated Parmesan cheese
¼ cup (50 mL) chopped flat leaf (Italian) parsley
2 tbsp (30 mL) lemon juice
¼ cup (50 mL) sour cream
1 tbsp (15 mL) salt
¾ cup (175 mL) dried fine breadcrumbs
Seasoned flour mixture:
¼ cup (50 mL) flour
2 tbsp (30 mL) salt
1 tbsp (15 mL) garlic powder
2 tbsp (30 mL) black pepper
1 tbsp (15 mL) onion powder
2 tbsp (30 mL) dried dill
For breading:
2 eggs
1 tbsp (15 mL) water
¾ cup (175 mL) dried fine breadcrumbs

For cooking:
vegetable oil

Peel and cube potatoes. In large pot, cover potatoes with cold water and bring to boil, cooking until easily pierced with knife. Drain and mash.

In small pan, melt butter over medium heat. Add onions, celery, bell peppers and garlic, cooking until softened but not browned. Remove from heat and set aside.

In large bowl, combine crab meat, green onions, Parmesan, parsley and lemon juice. Add cooled onions, celery, bell peppers and garlic. Add salt and breadcrumbs. Fold in sour cream.

Form into patties and refrigerate.

In separate bowl, prepare the seasoned flour: combine flour, salt, garlic powder, black pepper, onion powder and dried dill.

In another bowl, whisk eggs and water.

Set up breading station: 3 bowls from left to right, first seasoned flour, then egg mixture, then breadcrumbs. Dip the patties in flour, shake off excess; dip in egg mixture, then coat in breadcrumbs.

In large skillet, heat oil over medium heat. Sauté until golden brown on each side, turning once.

10 fishcakes / 5 servings

Suggested sauce: Lemon Dill Mayonnaise (see page 11)

Dungeness Crab Cakes

Bishop's Restaurant, Vancouver, BC

For a variation on this crab cake, try adding baby shrimp and barbecued salmon. Chef John Bishop emphasizes that the flavour is much better when the salmon is grilled rather than poached.

1 lb (455 g) cooked Dungeness crab meat
½ cup (125 mL) fresh breadcrumbs
1 egg
½ cup (125 mL) mayonnaise
2 tbsp (30 mL) chopped green onions
2 tbsp (30 mL) chopped fresh parsley
2 tbsp (30 mL) chopped fresh basil
1 lemon, zest and juice
Salt and freshly ground black pepper
For breading:
½ cup (125 mL) cornmeal
½ cup (125 mL) breadcrumbs
For cooking:
vegetable oil

Combine crab meat, ½ cup (125 mL) breadcrumbs, egg, mayonnaise, green onions, parsley, basil, lemon zest and juice in bowl. Season with salt and pepper to taste. Form into patties and refrigerate until chilled.

For breading, place cornmeal and ½ cup (125 mL) breadcrumbs in blender or food processor and mix well until crumbs are fine.

Coat patties with breading.

Heat vegetable oil in large frying pan on medium-high heat. Fry until golden and warmed through, about 5 minutes each side.

4 fishcakes / 2 servings

Suggested sauce: Pear Cranberry Chutney

Pear Cranberry Chutney
1 small red onion, diced
½ cup (125 mL) sugar
1 cup (250 mL) apple cider vinegar
1 tbsp (15 mL) grated fresh ginger
1 garlic clove, minced
4 pears, peeled and cored
1 cup (250 mL) dried cranberries
1 cinnamon stick

This chutney can be made with whatever fruit is in season, and will keep in the refrigerator for several weeks.

Combine onion, sugar, apple cider vinegar, ginger and garlic in saucepan. Bring to boil on medium-high heat, then add pears, dried cranberries and cinnamon stick. Turn heat to medium and simmer, covered, until fruit is tender, about 25 minutes. Cool, then remove and discard cinnamon stick.

Serve at room temperature.

Nancy's Amazing Crab Cakes

Hatfield Heritage Inn, Hartland, NB

These crab cakes offer a pleasing contrast in texture by combining a wonderfully crisp crust with a deliciously moist interior. It may take a little practise to get the balance just right, says Chef Richard Boulier, but making sure the pan is not too hot by heating the oil slowly will get you off to a good start.

4 tbsp (60 mL) butter
¼ cup (50 mL) flour
1 cup (250 mL) milk
½ tsp (2 mL) cayenne pepper
½ tsp (2 mL) salt
1 lb (455 g) crab meat
¼ cup (50 mL) finely chopped parsley
¼ cup (50 mL) finely chopped green onions
For breading:
3 eggs
3 cups (750 mL) fresh breadcrumbs
For cooking:
6 tbsp (90 mL) butter
2 tbsp (30 mL) vegetable oil

In heavy saucepan, melt 4 tbsp (60 mL) of butter over moderate heat. Add flour and mix well, cooking a few minutes to be sure flour is cooked.* Stirring constantly with wire whisk, add milk in a slow steady stream and cook until mixture comes to a boil. Reduce heat to low and simmer uncovered 2 to 3 minutes. The sauce should have the consistency of yogurt.

Stir in cayenne pepper and salt.

Scrape contents of saucepan into large mixing bowl. Add crab, parsley and green onions, and combine all ingredients thoroughly.

Refrigerate until mixture is completely cooled.

Form into patties and prepare breading.

Whisk eggs in small bowl. Dip patties into egg, then coat with breadcrumbs.

In heavy skillet, melt butter and vegetable oil and heat.

Add crab cakes, cooking until both sides are golden brown.

5 fishcakes / 2-3 servings

Suggested sauce: Lemon Dill Cream Sauce (see page 45)

*This is called a roux, which is equal parts by volume of fat and flour, cooked. It is more commonly used as a thickener in soups and stews.

Crab Cakes

Inn on the Cove, Saint John, NB

Chef Ross Mavis serves this fish cake at breakfast or lunch. Willa, his wife and business partner, claims it is the best crab cake she has ever eaten. It is very easy to prepare and is best cooked in a well-seasoned cast-iron frying pan with a little canola oil. A non-stick pan will do as well.

2 cups (500 mL) cooked crab meat, drained
1 egg yolk
1 cup (250 mL) fresh breadcrumbs
3 tbsp (45 mL) flour
2 tsp (10 mL) Worcestershire sauce
4 tbsp (60 mL) mayonnaise
1 clove garlic, minced
2 green onions, minced
4 tbsp (60 mL) chopped fresh parsley
1 tsp (5 mL) paprika
salt and pepper
For cooking:
canola oil

In bowl, mix crab and egg yolk. Add breadcrumbs, flour, Worcestershire sauce, mayonnaise, garlic, green onions, parsley and paprika.

Season with salt and pepper to taste.

Form into patties.

Add canola oil to hot pan and cook until golden brown, about 2 minutes each side.

4 fishcakes / 2 servings

Suggested sauce: Cajun Rémoulade

Cajun Rémoulade (author's recipe)
1 Basic Mayonnaise (see page 11)
2 tbsp (30 mL) grainy mustard
2 tbsp (30 mL) chopped capers
½ tsp (2 mL) cayenne pepper
1 tbsp (15 mL) chopped fresh parsley
1 tbsp (15 mL) lemon juice
1 tbsp (15 mL) red wine vinegar
salt and pepper to taste

Rémoulade is a classic French sauce. This version has cayenne to give it heat.

To Basic Mayonnaise recipe, add ingredients shown above.

Potato-Crusted Snow Crab Cakes

Chives Canadian Bistro, Halifax, NS

Chef Darren Lewis says, "This recipe is an original; the crust doesn't come from the traditional breadcrumbs. It is made from potato flakes. We have the luxury of living close to the ocean. The crab comes directly from the shores of Cape Breton or northern New Brunswick."

2 tbsp (30 mL) butter
½ cup (125 mL) diced red onions
½ cup (125 mL) diced celery
1 lb (455 g) snow crab leg meat
1 cup (250 mL) fresh breadcrumbs
½ cup (125 mL) diced red peppers
2 egg yolks
¼ cup (50 mL) chopped chives

½ tsp (2 mL) hot pepper sauce
1 tsp (5 mL) Worcestershire sauce
1 ½ tsp (7 mL) salt
1 tsp (5 mL) pepper
For breading:
3 egg yolks
¼ cup (50 mL) buttermilk
1 cup (250 mL) flour
1 cup (250 mL) potato flakes
For cooking:
vegetable oil

Melt butter in skillet over medium heat; cook red onions and celery until softened but not browned. In large bowl, combine crab, 1 cup (250 mL) breadcrumbs, red onions, red peppers, celery, 2 egg yolks, chives, hot pepper sauce, Worcestershire sauce, salt and pepper in bowl. Form into patties and refrigerate until well chilled.

Mix 3 egg yolks and buttermilk. Set up breading station: 3 bowls left to right, first flour, then egg yolk mixture, then potato flakes. Dip cakes in flour, shake off excess; dip in egg yolk mixture, then coat in potato flakes.

Deep fry at 350°F (180°C) until golden brown.

5 fishcakes / 2-3 servings

Serving suggestions: Chives' Sour Cream, Pickled Red Onions

Chives' Sour Cream
1 cup (250 mL) sour cream
1 tbsp (15 mL) prepared horseradish
1 tbsp (15 mL) grainy Dijon mustard
1 tbsp (15 mL) minced shallots
¼ cup (60 mL) chopped chives
salt and fresh cracked pepper to taste

Combine all ingredients and let stand refrigerated overnight for best flavour.

Pickled Red Onions
1 large red onion
1 cup (250 mL) red wine vinegar
1 cup (250 mL) brown sugar
2 tbsp (30 mL) sea salt
1 tbsp (15 mL) black pepper
1 bay leaf
1 tbsp (15 mL) grenadine (for colour, may be omitted)

Slice onion into rings and set aside in glass container.

In saucepan, bring red wine vinegar, brown sugar, sea salt, black pepper, bay leaf and grenadine to boil.

Pour boiling mixture over onions in glass container, making sure onions are completely submersed in liquid.

Refrigerate overnight.

Drain and serve onions as garnish or side dish.

Thai Crab Cakes

RainCoast Café, Tofino, BC

Bean sprouts give a bit of crunch to these cakes, both inside and out. RainCoast owner Lisa Henderson mentions that for a similar effect you can substitute daikon — a white radish. Oyster sauce adds depth and a hint of sweetness to the crab cakes.

2 lbs (900 g) cooked halibut or cod (or other white fish)
1 lb (455 g) crab meat
1 ¼ cups (300 mL) panko breadcrumbs
1 cup (250 mL) fresh bean sprouts, coarsely chopped
¼ cup (50 mL) finely chopped green onions
¼ cup (50 mL) finely chopped fresh cilantro
2 tbsp (30 mL) fresh lime juice
⅛ tsp (0.5 mL) red pepper flakes
1 tsp (5 mL) oyster sauce
1 large egg
For cooking:
canola oil

In large mixing bowl, combine fish, crab, breadcrumbs, bean sprouts, green onions, cilantro, lime juice, red pepper flakes, oyster sauce and egg. Mix well, form into patties and refrigerate for several hours.

Sauté in canola oil over medium-high heat until golden brown on both sides, turning once.

8 fishcakes / 4 servings

Suggested sauce: Lemon Aïoli (see page 85)

Cod

The commerce of the East Coast was built on the currency of cod; for years it was the most important catch. Cod is a lean, white-fleshed fish with a mild flavour and is usually sold as fillets. It is the basis of traditional fishcakes. Let odour be your guide when buying fresh cod. It should have a clean and slightly salty smell. Check for worms — small reddish-brown parasites that tend to turn up more frequently in cod caught in warm waters. Unappetizing, but not harmful, any worms can be removed and discarded.

Fresh fish should be used soon after buying. It may be kept, tightly wrapped and refrigerated, for a couple of days. When buying frozen cod, look for signs of freezer burn and avoid packages that have a lot of frost under the wrap. Thaw in the refrigerator, and handle as fresh once thawed.

Blackened Fishcakes

Gaffer's Bistro, Whitehall Country Inn,
Clarenville, NFLD

Blackening spice gives the cakes a dark red hue.
Combined with the cucumber corn chutney,
with hints of green, yellow and purple, this
makes a very colourful and spicy meal.

6 oz (170 g) fresh cod fillets
2 cups (500 mL) mashed potatoes (1 lb/455 g/
 about 10 medium peeled potatoes)
1 tbsp (15 mL) butter
½ cup (125 mL) finely chopped onions
½ cup (125 mL) finely chopped celery
2 tsp (10 mL) salt
1 tsp (5 mL) white pepper
Blackening blend:
2 ½ tbsp (30 mL) paprika
1 tsp (5 mL) garlic powder
1 tsp (5 mL) onion powder
1 tsp (5 mL) white pepper
1 tsp (5 mL) black pepper
1 tsp (5 mL) cayenne pepper
1 tsp (5 mL) cumin
1 tsp (5 mL) curry powder
For cooking:
olive oil

Bring saucepan or deep skillet of water to boil;
turn heat to medium and place cod in pan,
ensuring water covers fish. Cook until cod is well
done and flakes apart easily, drain and let cool.

Peel and cube potatoes. In large pot, cover
potatoes with cold water and bring to boil until
easily pierced with knife. Drain and mash.

In a skillet, melt butter, sauté onions and celery
until softened but not brown.

Combine cod, potatoes, onions, celery, salt and
pepper in bowl. Form into patties.

Chilling in refrigerator before cooking will help
the fishcakes keep their shape while cooking.

Combine blackening spices in glass jar and
shake well to mix thoroughly.

Immediately prior to cooking, dust each cake with blackened seasoning.

Preheat oven to 400°F (200°C). Heat olive oil in cast-iron frying pan until very hot but not smoking. Gently place each cake in oil and cook 3 to 4 minutes each side to allow blackening to occur. Remove from pan; finish cooking in oven for 12 to 15 minutes until cakes are heated through.

5 fishcakes / 2-3 servings

Suggested sauce: Cucumber Corn Chutney

Cucumber Corn Chutney

2 ears of fresh corn (or 1 cup (250 mL) frozen or
    canned kernels)
1 large cucumber, peeled, seeded and diced
1 small red onion, diced
1 medium tomato, seeded and diced
⅓ cup (75 mL) chopped fresh cilantro
1 tsp (5 mL) salt
1 tsp (5 mL) pepper

In boiling water, cook corn for 8 to 10 minutes. Allow to cool and remove kernels from cob.

In bowl, combine corn, cucumber, onion, tomato, cilantro, salt and pepper.

Serve chilled.

Dungeness Crab and Ling Cod Brandade

The Aerie, Malahat, BC

Chef Chris Jones says that this is a variation on a dish traditionally eaten in France. While these cakes are served cold and made with crab meat and fresh ling cod, in France the dish is served warm with salad and is made with Atlantic cod.

1 cup (250 mL) milk
1 sprig fresh thyme
1 bay leaf
3 whole peppercorns
1 garlic clove, whole
¼ cup (60 mL) peeled and sliced potato (65 g/ about ½ medium potato)
6 oz (170 g) ling cod (or any white fish)
4 oz (115 g) crab meat
2 tbsp (30 mL) olive oil
For breading:
4 tbsp (60 mL) flour
1 egg
2 tbsp (30 mL) olive oil
1 cup (250 mL) plus 2 tbsp (30 mL) milk
1 tbsp (15 mL) porphyra seaweed (or dried nori flakes)
1 tbsp (15 mL) sesame seeds
For cooking:
sesame oil

In heavy-bottomed pot, bring to boil 1 cup (250 mL) milk, thyme, bay leaf, peppercorns and garlic.

Add sliced potato and ling cod.

Simmer for 5 minutes over medium heat, set aside to cool.

When cool, remove thyme stem, bay leaf, garlic and peppercorns. Drain liquid.

Combine fish-potato mixture with crab and 2 tbsp (30 mL) of olive oil.

Shape into patties and refrigerate until chilled.

Beat egg with remaining 2 tbsp (30 mL) olive oil and 2 tbsp (30 mL) milk.

In separate bowl, combine seaweed and sesame seeds. Set up breading station: 3 bowls left to right, first flour, then egg mixture, then seaweed mixture. Dip patties in flour, shake off excess; dip in egg mixture then coat in seaweed mixture.

Sauté in sesame oil over medium-high heat until golden brown on both sides, turning once.

4 fishcakes / 2 servings

Suggested sauce: Lemon-Cilantro Broth

Lemon-Cilantro Broth

¾ cup fish stock (175 mL)
½ tbsp (10 mL) chopped lemon grass
1 tbsp (15 mL) lemon juice
3 tbsp (45 mL) soy sauce
3 tbsp (45 mL) sesame oil
1 tsp (5 mL) chopped fresh cilantro
1 tbsp (15 mL) finely chopped lemon zest

In a pan over medium-high heat, bring to boil stock, lemon grass and lemon juice. Continue cooking until reduced by one third. Whisk in soy sauce and sesame oil. Add cilantro and lemon zest.

Traditional Breaded Fishcakes

Gaffer's Bistro, Whitehall Country Inn,
Clarenville, NFLD

Chef Chris Sheppard says that this recipe can be prepared ahead and frozen. When unexpected company arrive, you can impress them with an instant fishcake meal.

5 oz (145 g) fresh cod
2 cups (500 mL) mashed potatoes (1 lb/455 g/
    about 10 medium peeled potatoes)
1 tbsp (15 mL) butter
½ cup (125 mL) finely diced onions
½ cup (125 mL) finely diced celery
2 tsp (10 mL) salt
1 tsp (5 mL) white pepper
For breading:
2 eggs, beaten
¼ cup (50 mL) milk
1 cup (250 mL) flour
2 cups (500 mL) fine dry breadcrumbs
For cooking:
butter

Place cod in pan, cover with water and simmer 8 to 10 minutes over medium heat, until fish flakes apart easily.

Peel and cube potatoes. In large pot, cover potatoes with cold water and bring to boil, cooking until easily pierced with knife. Drain and mash.

In 1 tbsp (15 mL) of butter, sauté onions and celery until soft.

In large bowl, combine cod, potatoes, onions, celery, salt and pepper.

Let cool, and form into patties.

Combine eggs and milk.

Set up breading station: 3 bowls left to right, first flour, then egg mixture, then breadcrumbs. Dip cakes in flour, shake off excess; dip in egg mixture, then coat in breadcrumbs.

Pan-fry in butter until golden brown on each side.

12 fishcakes / 6 servings

Salt Cod

Once a staple in Atlantic Canadian households, salt cod is traditional for fishcakes. Sides of salt cod can be found in specialty markets. In supermarkets it is possible to buy bags or small boxes of salt cod bits. With the cod fishery diminishing yearly, packages of mixed salt fish are more widely available. This mix of cod, haddock and other white fish is an excellent substitute.

When using any salt fish, soak it in cold water for several hours, changing the water four or five times to get rid of the excess salt.

Codfish Cakes

Spot O'Tea Restaurant, Stanley Bridge, PEI

This simple fishcake is the quintessential Maritime cod cake and Spot O'Tea's signature dish.

16 oz (455 g) salt cod
4 cups (950 mL) mashed potatoes (2 lbs/900 g/ about 20 medium peeled potatoes)
1 cup (250 mL) finely diced onions
½ tsp (2 mL) dried summer savoury
salt and pepper to taste

Soak fish 8 to 10 hours in cold water, changing water 4 to 5 times.

Boil fish until tender and flaky, 15 to 20 minutes.

Peel and cube potatoes. In large pot, cover potatoes with cold water and bring to boil, cooking until easily pierced with knife. Drain and mash.

In large bowl, combine potatoes, fish, onions and savoury.

Season to taste, being careful not to over salt.

Let cool and form into patties.

Pan-fry in butter or oil until golden brown.

8 fishcakes / 4 servings

Suggested sauce: Tomato Chow Chow

Tomato Chow Chow *(author's recipe)*

6 cups (1.5 L) chopped ripe tomatoes
3 cups (750 mL) chopped onions
½ cup (125 mL) finely chopped sweet peppers
    (green, red, yellow or a combination)
¼ cup (60 mL) salt
2 cups (500 mL) white vinegar
2 cups (500 mL) water
½ cup (125 mL) pickling spice
1 cup (250 mL) sugar

Wash and roughly chop tomatoes. In large bowl, combine tomatoes, onions and peppers. Sprinkle with salt and let stand, covered, at room temperature for several hours.

After standing, drain excess liquid. Rinse well and place in large pot.

Add vinegar and water. Place pickling spice in a cheesecloth bag or tea ball and immerse in pot with vegetable mixture. Cook over medium heat until vegetables are soft, then add sugar. Continue cooking for 30 to 45 minutes.

Remove spice bag. Pour chow chow in containers and refrigerate until ready to use.

Mom's Fishcakes

Castle Rock Country Inn, Ingonish Ferry, NS

Castle Rock's chef, Ian MacLellan, says that if the onions are gently fried until they are caramelized, you will add wonderful flavour to your fishcakes.

8 oz (225 g) salt cod
2 cups (500 mL) mashed potatoes (1 lb/455 g/ about 10 medium peeled potatoes)
1 ½ cups (375 mL) finely diced onions
3 tbsp (45 mL) butter
½ tsp (2 mL) dried sage
pepper to taste

Soak fish 8 to 10 hours in cold water, changing water 4 to 5 times.

Boil fish until tender and flaky, 15 to 20 minutes.

Peel and cube potatoes. In large pot, cover potatoes with cold water and bring to boil, cooking until easily pierced with knife. Drain and mash.

In large bowl, combine potatoes, fish, onions, butter and sage.

Season to taste, being careful not to over salt.

Let cool and form into patties.

Pan-fry in butter or oil until golden brown.

4 fishcakes / 2 servings

Suggested sauce: Mustard Pickles

Mustard Pickles

1 large cauliflower
2 lbs (900 g) onions, peeled and chopped
3 large cucumbers, chopped
1 red pepper, chopped
4 cups (1 L) cold water
¼ cup (60 mL) salt
4 cups (1 L) white vinegar
2 ½ cups (625 mL) white sugar
¼ cup (60 mL) water
½ cup (125 mL) cornstarch
3 tbsp (45 mL) dry mustard
1 tbsp (15 mL) turmeric

Remove florets from cauliflower and chop roughly into medium pieces. In large pot, place cauliflower, onions, cucumber and red pepper. Cover with cold water, stir in salt and let stand for several hours at room temperature.

After standing, place vegetable pot on stove and bring to boil. Cook until vegetables are softened.

While vegetables are cooking, in second pot heat vinegar, stir in sugar to dissolve. Make a paste of ¼ cup (50 mL) water, dry mustard, cornstarch and turmeric. Add this paste to sugar-vinegar water and boil until thickened.

Drain vegetables and pour vinegar mixture over the hot vegetables. Stir together then pour into jars for canning or refrigerate until ready to use.

Salt Cod Brandade

Inn at Bay Fortune, Bay Fortune, PEI

In this recipe Chef Gordon Bailey adds two aromatic herbs — anise and thyme – that release their flavour while the fish is being poached. The wonderfully mellow background flavour to the fishcakes is reminiscent of the French Mediterranean.

1 lb (455 g) salt cod
2 cups (500 mL) milk
1 clove garlic, crushed
1 pod star anise
½ cup (125 mL) flat leaf (Italian) parsley, chopped
1 tsp (5 mL) fresh thyme
½ lb (225 g) Yukon Gold potatoes (about 5 medium peeled potatoes)
1 tbsp (15 mL) extra-virgin olive oil
2 cups (500 mL) whipping cream (35%)
2 cups (500 mL) cream
salt and pepper to taste
1 cup (250 mL) flour
For cooking:
butter or oil

Soak fish 8 to 10 hours in cold water, changing water 4 to 5 times.

Place cod in heavy-bottomed pot, cover with milk and add garlic, star anise, parsley and thyme.

Heat to simmer and let the flavours blend. Set aside.

Peel and slice potatoes. Place in a heavy-bottomed pot over medium heat.

Add ½ the olive oil and stir with wooden spoon until potato slices are evenly coated with oil.

Add cream to potatoes, stirring every few minutes until potatoes have broken down into a purée (30 to 45 minutes), set aside.

Remove cod from poaching liquid, discard everything but cod, and flake cod into puréed potatoes, stirring constantly. Season with salt and pepper.

Place mixture in square cake pan and refrigerate for several hours or overnight.

When set, invert cake pan over cutting board to turn out mixture.

Cut into squares.

Dust with flour and pan-fry in butter or oil until golden brown.

6 fishcakes / 3 servings

Suggested sauce: Chive Crème Fraîche

Chive Crème Fraîche

½ cup (125 mL) whipping cream (35%)
1 tbsp (15 mL) buttermilk
1 lemon, juiced
2 tbsp (30 mL) fresh chives, chopped
salt and white pepper to taste

In glass bottle with lid, combine cream, buttermilk and lemon juice and let stand at room temperature for 8 to 24 hours until thickened.

Remove mixture from container and add chives, salt and pepper.

Refrigerate.

Crème fraîche is a mature, thickened cream. It can be boiled without curdling for a hot sauce, and lends itself to all kinds of variations. Use whatever fresh herbs are on hand.

Cape Breton Fishcakes

Keltic Lodge, Ingonish, NS

8 oz (250 g) salt cod
3 cups (700 mL) mashed potatoes (1 ½ lb/750 g/
  about 15 medium peeled potatoes)
½ cup (125 mL) finely diced salt pork fat
1 cup (250 mL) finely diced onions
½ cup (125 mL) finely diced celery
½ tsp (2 mL) fresh thyme
½ tsp (2 mL) summer savoury
salt and pepper to taste
Fresh chopped chives for garnish

Soak fish 8 to 10 hours in cold water, changing water 4 to 5 times.

Boil fish until tender and flaky, 15 to 20 minutes.

Peel and cube potatoes. In large pot, cover potatoes with cold water and bring to boil, cooking until easily pierced with knife. Drain and mash.

Sauté pork fat until fat is rendered out and pieces start to harden. Add onions and celery and cook until soft.

Remove from heat; add thyme and savoury and stir.

Drain excess fat from celery, onion, herb and salt pork mixture.

In large bowl, combine mixture with potatoes and fish. Season to taste, being careful not to over salt.

Let cool and form into patties.

Pan-fry in butter or oil until golden brown.

6 fishcakes / 3 servings

Suggested sauce: Lemon Herb Butter Sauce

Lemon Herb Butter Sauce

¾ cup (175 mL) dry white wine
1 tbsp (15 mL) lemon juice
½ tbsp (10 mL) chopped shallots
¾ cup (175 mL) whipping cream (35%)
1 cup (250 mL) unsalted butter, cubed
¼ cup (60 mL) fresh chopped herbs (such as
  parsley or tarragon)
salt and black pepper to taste

Put white wine, lemon juice and shallots in saucepan over medium-high heat. Cook until wine is nearly evaporated. Stir in cream and continue cooking for another 5 minutes.

Turn heat down to medium and begin dropping in butter cubes slowly, one at a time, whisking each one into the sauce. After all butter has been added, remove from heat, add herbs, then salt and pepper to taste and serve immediately.

Fishcakes

Seawind Landing Country Inn, Charlos Cove, NS

At Seawind Landing, these authentic Maritime fishcakes are served for a hearty breakfast.

16 oz (455 g) salt cod
4 cups (950 mL) mashed potatoes (2 lbs/900 g/ about 20 medium peeled potatoes)
1 ½ cups (375 mL) finely diced onions
2 tbsp (30 mL) butter
¼ tsp (1 mL) dried summer savoury
½ tsp (2 mL) dried thyme
½ tsp (2 mL) dried parsley
1 egg
pepper to taste

Soak fish 8 to 10 hours in cold water, changing water 4 to 5 times.

Boil fish until tender and flaky, 15 to 20 minutes.

Peel and cube potatoes. In large pot, cover potatoes with cold water and bring to boil, cooking until easily pierced with knife. Drain and mash.

Sauté onions in butter until soft. Set aside.

In large bowl, combine potatoes, fish, onions, savoury, thyme, parsley and egg.

Season to taste, being careful not to over salt.

Let cool and form into patties.

Pan-fry in butter or oil until golden brown.

8 fishcakes / 4 servings

Fishcakes

Inn on the Lake, Fall River, NS

Chef Darrell MacMullin is from Cape Breton and was introduced to fishcakes by his grandmother. Like many other chefs, the fishcake on his menu was introduced as a special but became so popular it is now a regular item on the brunch menu.

2 lbs (900 g) salt cod
2 cups (500 mL) mashed potatoes (1 lb/455 g/
  about 10 medium peeled potatoes)
3 tbsp (45 mL) butter
2 cups (500 mL) finely diced Spanish onions
1 egg
salt and pepper to taste
For cooking:
butter or oil

Soak fish 8 to 10 hours in cold water, changing water 4 to 5 times.

Boil fish until tender and flaky, 15 to 20 minutes.

Peel and cube potatoes. In large pot, cover potatoes with cold water and bring to boil, cooking until easily pierced with knife. Drain and mash with butter.

In large bowl, combine potatoes, fish, onions and egg.

Season to taste, being careful not to over salt.

Let cool and form into patties.

Pan-fry in butter or oil until golden brown.

12 fishcakes / 6 servings

Haddock & Sablefish

In addition to cod, there are many kinds of white fish available. The most popular are haddock and halibut. Sablefish, ling cod and hake are also good choices. These are all mild-tasting fish and can be substituted one for another.

When buying whole fish, look for shiny scales and bright eyes. If the fish is already filleted, check for smell — there shouldn't be a strong fishy aroma. To get the best fish, find a reliable source with high turnover and knowledgeable staff. Buy fresh in season. When buying frozen, beware of signs of freezer burn or frost in the package.

Smoked Sablefish Cakes

Café Brio, Victoria, BC

Sablefish is the Canadian term for black cod. The high fat content gives these fish more flavour than other white fish. They are ideal for smoking.

4 cups (950 mL) mashed Yukon Gold potatoes (2 lbs/ 900 g/ about 20 medium peeled potatoes)
½ cup (125 mL) unsalted butter
1 tsp (5 mL) minced garlic
½ cup (125 mL) whipping cream (35%)
3 sprigs fresh thyme
8 oz (225 g) naturally smoked sablefish (black cod)
1 egg yolk
1 tsp (5 mL) salt
1 tsp (5 mL) pepper
For breading:
2 eggs
½ cup (125 mL) milk
1 cup (250 mL) flour
2 cups (500 mL) fresh breadcrumbs
For cooking:
vegetable oil

Peel and cube potatoes. In large pot, cover potatoes with cold water and bring to boil, cooking until easily pierced with knife. Drain and mash.

In large skillet, heat butter. Sauté garlic until soft, add cream, thyme and sablefish and simmer until fish begins to fall apart. Remove from heat and remove thyme stems and any fish bones. Strain and reserve liquid.

In large bowl, combine fish and potatoes. Pour in enough of reserved liquid to bring mixture together. Add egg yolk, salt and pepper.

Form into patties and refrigerate until cool.

Whisk eggs and milk.

Set up breading station: 3 bowls left to right, first flour, then egg mixture, then breadcrumbs. Dip patties in flour, shake off excess; dip in egg mixture then coat in breadcrumbs.

In heavy skillet, heat vegetable oil. Sauté over medium heat until golden brown.

10 fishcakes / 5 servings

Suggested sauce: Lemon Aïoli

Lemon Aïoli

1 egg yolk

1 tsp (5 mL) Dijon mustard

½ clove garlic, chopped

1 tsp (5 mL) chopped capers

2 tsp (10 mL) lemon zest

¾ cup (180 mL) canola oil

3 tbsp (45 mL) lemon juice

4 tsp (20 mL) chopped fresh dill

½ tsp (3 mL) Tabasco sauce

½ tsp (3 mL) salt

¼ tsp (1 mL) white pepper

In large stainless steel bowl, whisk egg yolk, Dijon mustard, garlic, chopped capers and lemon zest.

While whisking, very slowly drizzle in canola oil. As the aïoli thickens, alternate with lemon juice until all oil and juice has been incorporated.

Add chopped dill, Tabasco sauce, salt and white pepper.

Fish-Leek Cakes

Hillcroft Café and Guest House, Lunenburg, NS

Don't skip the pungent Thai fish sauce; it adds a subtle flavour that makes these cakes unique.

1 lb (455 g) haddock fillets
2 cups (500 mL) mashed potatoes (1 lb/455 g/ about 10 medium peeled potatoes)
¼ cup (50 mL) melted butter
2 cups finely sliced leeks*
2 eggs
1 tbsp (15 mL) Thai fish sauce
2 tsp (10 mL) finely chopped parsley
1 tsp (5 mL) paprika
½ tsp (2 mL) cayenne pepper

1 tsp (5 mL) salt
½ tsp (2 mL) black pepper
For breading:
3 eggs
2 tbsp (30 mL) vegetable oil
1 cup (250 mL) flour
1 cup (250 mL) fresh breadcrumbs
1 cup (250 mL) cornmeal
For cooking:
vegetable oil

Bring saucepan or deep skillet of water to a boil; turn heat to medium and place haddock in pan, ensuring water covers fish. Cook until haddock is well done and flakes apart easily. Set aside to cool.

Peel and cube potatoes. In large pot, cover potatoes with cold water and bring to boil, cooking until easily pierced with knife. Drain and mash.

In melted butter, sauté leeks until softened but not brown. Set aside.

In large bowl, combine fish, potatoes, leeks, butter, 2 eggs, Thai fish sauce, parsley, paprika, cayenne, salt and pepper.

Form into patties and refrigerate until well chilled.

Beat 3 eggs with oil. Combine cornmeal and breadcrumbs. Dredge patties in flour, then egg wash, then cornmeal/breadcrumb mixture.

Heat oil in large skillet over medium heat. Add fishcakes (oil should come halfway up the sides of the cakes). Fry until both sides are golden, drain on paper towels.

10 fishcakes / 5 servings

Suggested sauce: Hollandaise Sauce

*To prepare leeks for cooking, split lengthwise in quarters and spread layers apart to wash thoroughly. We use both the white and green parts.

Hollandaise Sauce *(author's recipe)*

1 lb (455 g) warm clarified butter (see page 17)
¼ tsp (1 mL) salt
¼ tsp (1 mL) pepper
3 tbsp (45 mL) white vinegar (or white wine vinegar)
2 tbsp (30 mL) cold water
16 egg yolks

2 tbsp (30 mL) lemon juice

Combine salt, pepper and vinegar in saucepan and reduce until nearly dry. Remove from heat and add cold water.

Transfer to stainless steel bowl.

Add egg yolks to bowl, and beat well using wire whisk.

Hold bowl over a hot water bath (double boiler) and continue to beat yolks until thick and creamy.

Remove bowl from heat. Slowly and gradually beat in the warm, clarified butter, adding butter drop by drop at first.

If sauce becomes too thick, beat in a little lemon juice.

When all butter has been added, add remaining lemon juice.

Taste and add more salt and pepper if you like. Serve immediately.

Seafood Cakes

Marshlands Inn, Sackville, NB

Chef Roger says this recipe can be made thick for a main course, or thinner to serve as an appetizer. If you find the cakes too crumbly, he suggests adding another egg and more breadcrumbs to bind the seafood.

4 oz (115 g) Chinese noodles (or rice vermicelli)
4 oz (115 g) haddock
1oz (30 g) scallops
1 oz (30 g) shrimp
8 tsp (40 mL) chopped green onions
3 tbsp (45 mL) butter
2 oz (60 g) lobster meat
½ cup (125 mL) grated asiago cheese
1 tsp (5 mL) salt
1 tsp (5 mL) pepper
2 tbsp (30 mL) fresh parsley
8 tbsp (120 mL) fresh breadcrumbs
2 eggs
For cooking:
vegetable oil

Cook noodles until tender. Rinse and chop into 2-inch pieces. Set aside.

Sauté haddock, scallops, shrimp and green onions in butter until just cooked. Add lobster to seafood mixture and let cool.

In large bowl, combine seafood and green onions, noodles, cheese, salt, pepper, parsley, breadcrumbs and eggs.

Form into patties.

In a non-stick pan over medium-high heat, cook in oil until golden brown on both sides.

4 fishcakes / 2 servings

Suggested sauce: Jalapeño Jelly

Jalapeño Jelly
¼ cup (50 mL) chopped fresh jalapeños*
¾ cup (175 mL) chopped red pepper
1 cup (250 mL) white vinegar
3 tbsp (45 mL) lemon juice
5 cups (1250 mL) white sugar
6 oz (170 g) Certo (fruit pectin)

Wearing gloves, slice jalapeños in half lengthwise and scrape out seeds. In blender, process jalapeños, red pepper and ½ cup (125 mL) vinegar until smooth. Pour into saucepan; add remaining vinegar, lemon juice, sugar and Certo. Bring to boil and cook 10 minutes. Remove from heat and skim.

Cool and store in Mason jars.

*If fresh jalapeños are unavailable, use ¼ cup (50 mL) chopped canned jalapeños.

Smoked Sablefish Cakes

Metropolitan Hotel, Vancouver, BC

Chef Baechler explains that cooked sablefish has a light butter flavour and flaky texture which is similar to sea bass. Sablefish is flash-frozen immediately on the boats to preserve freshness. "Nothing beats fresh fish," says the chef, "but with this freezing technique, you can hardly taste the difference." He suggests making the fishcakes the morning before you serve them and chill them in the refrigerator.

2 cups (500 mL) warm mashed potatoes (1 lb/
   455 g/about 10 medium peeled potatoes)
½ lb (225 g) cooked flaked smoked sablefish
1 tbsp (15 mL) chopped fresh cilantro
1 tbsp (15 mL) chopped fresh chives
1 tbsp (15 mL) butter, melted
salt
pepper
lemon juice
For breading:
1 egg
3 tbsp (45 mL) cold water
1 cup (250 mL) panko breadcrumbs
For cooking:
olive oil

Peel and cube potatoes. In large pot, cover potatoes with cold water and bring to boil, cooking until easily pierced with knife. Drain and mash.

In large mixing bowl, combine potatoes, fish, cilantro, chives and butter; season with salt, pepper and lemon juice to taste.

Form into patties and refrigerate for at least 1 hour.

Whisk egg with cold water in bowl. Gently dip patties, one by one, in the egg mixture to coat both sides. Transfer to breadcrumbs and coat well.

In shallow non-stick pan, lightly brown in olive oil on medium heat.

6 fishcakes / 3 servings

Suggested sauce: Red and Green Tomato Salsa

Red and Green Tomato Salsa

1 tsp (5 mL) olive oil
½ sweet red pepper, diced
½ fresh jalapeno pepper, seeded and diced (see
   page 22)
2 plum tomatoes, seeded and diced
3 small green tomatoes, seeded and diced
⅓ cup (115 mL) chopped fresh coriander
¼ tsp (1 mL) ground coriander
1 tbsp (5 mL) lime juice
1 tsp (5 mL) hot pepper sauce
salt and pepper to taste

Gently toss all ingredients in large glass bowl, refrigerate and allow flavours to blend, up to 4 hours.

Dungeness Crab and
Sablefish Cakes

Kingfisher Resort and Spa, Courtenay, BC

26 oz (750 g) Dungeness crab meat
11 oz (300 g) sablefish fillet, cooked
3 tbsp (45 mL) chopped green onion
¼ cup (50 mL) diced sweet red pepper
2 tbsp (30 mL) mayonnaise
1 egg
For breading:
2 tsp (10 mL) black pepper
1 tsp (5 mL) chili pepper flakes
1 tbsp (15 mL) lemon zest
½ tsp (2 mL) sea salt
1 cup (250 mL) flour
½ cup (50 mL) cornmeal
2 eggs
2 tsp (10 mL) lemon juice
1 tsp (5 mL) Worcestershire sauce
2 cups (500 mL) panko breadcrumbs
For cooking:
2 tbsp (30 mL) olive oil
3 tbsp (45 mL) butter

In large mixing bowl, combine crab meat, sablefish, onions, red pepper, mayonnaise and 1 egg. Form into patties and refrigerate for at least 1 hour.

In spice grinder or clean coffee mill, grind black pepper, chili pepper flakes, lemon zest and sea salt. Add spice mix to flour and cornmeal in bowl.

In bowl, whisk 2 eggs with lemon juice and Worcestershire sauce. Set up breading station: 3 bowls left to right, first flour, then egg mixture, then breadcrumbs. Dip patties in flour, shake off excess; dip in egg mixture, then coat in breadcrumbs.

In non-stick skillet over medium heat, melt butter and oil. Sauté until golden brown on both sides, turning once.

10 fishcakes / 5 servings

Suggested sauce: Lemon Aïoli (see page 85)

Index

Photo Credits

Photography by Scott Munn with the following exceptions:

Pages 6, 34, 82 – Hamid Attie Photography. Pages 24, 58, 81 – Julian Beveridge. Page 77 – Martin Caird. Pages 5, 69, 79 — Cathy Carnahan. Page 43 – Andre Gallant. Page 53 – Keith Vaughan. Pages 8, 17, 23, 57, 89 – Janet Kimber. Pages 9, 11, 14, 15, 22, 25, 31, 37, 38, 39, 45, 49, 56, 67, 75, 93, 96 – Meghan Collins. Page 50 – Dwayne Coon.

Thank you to the Fishermen's Market, Halifax, for their assistance.

Cover photo: Hamid Attie Photography